A Phonetic English to Arawak Dictionary

Damon Corrie

Published by Damon Corrie, 2021.

A PHONETIC ENGLISH TO ARAWAK DICTIONARY

First edition. September 24, 2021.

ISBN: 979-8201102036

Written by Damon Corrie.

Table of Contents

I dedicate this book to my most beloved High School teacher and later Headmaster, who taught me History and social studies - Mr. Gregory Castagne, this is the ONE educator whom I can honestly credit - with having turned me from being a teenaged 'Rebel without a cause'...to an adult Rebel WITH a cause; and we remain friends to this day.

I also dedicate this book to Guyana Army Combat veteran - His Excellency Great Lokono Chief Leyland Clenkian, of the 240 square mile Pakuri Autonomous Territory, in Region 4, Guyana; who has been my personal friend and inspiration since 1992...and who personally performed the final edit of this book, being a fluent speaker himself.

DEDICATION

I dedicate this book to my most beloved High School teacher and later Headmaster, who taught me History and social studies - Mr Gregory Castagne, this is the ONE educator whom I can honestly credit - with having turned me from being a teenaged 'Rebel without a cause'...to an adult Rebel WITH a cause; and we remain friends to this day.

I also dedicate this book to Guyana Army Combat veteran - His Excellency Great Lokono Chief Leyland Clenkian, of the 240 square mile Pakuri Autonomous Territory, in Region 4, Guyana; who has been my personal friend and inspiration since 1992 - when he personally welcomed me back into the tribe, after a 67 year exile of my family clan bloodline from Guyana.

This is because in my own Eagle Clan (Bariria Korobado) of the Lokono people, after the measles & smallpox epidemics of the late 1800's, the only surviving member of our traditional hereditary ruling family (my great grandmother) emigrated into exile to Barbados in 1925 (and died there in 1928), with her 6 children. So the line of Hereditary Chiefs that spanned over 300 years - was broken; even though Great grandmother preserved the bloodline of her father, our last ruling Hereditary Chief - Amorotaheh Haubariria (Flying Harpy Eagle)...and there are now 100 of us Descendant-heirs in Barbados today, 100+ in the UK, 85 in Cuba, and about 40 of us in North America - all descended from the 6 children of Great grandmother, our Tribal Princess, even though there is no word equivalent for 'Prince' or 'Princess' in the Lokono language, one is just known as a son or daughter of the Hereditary Chief, that is all.

Chief Leyland (whom I respectfully call the Jaguar Chief - due to his renowned fearlessness) - is a fluent speaker of the Lokono language, and he kindly accepted to perform the final edit of this book before its September 2021 publication.

He was preceded by my Lokono father-in-law - elder & master traditional craftsman - Mr Joseph Simon, who was also a fluent speaker...but who unfortunately died in October 2020 before this book could be completed. He had encouraged me to begin this project - over 28 years ago, and this book is a result of those almost 3 decades of notes.

My still living fluent speaking Lokono mother-in-law Etheldreda Simon, and her fluent speaking brother Dunstan Andrews, both also contributed many words to this book.

CHAPTER 1 - INTRODUCTION

The absolute MOST IMPORTANT FACT you need to know, is that there is no 'right' way to write the Lokono-Arawak language, remember it was NEVER a written language, in fact I am the first person in the world to write my Tribal language PHONETICALLY - as people who speak English as their first language SHOULD pronounce it.

I say this because even though there is no 'right' way to write it - there IS a right way to PRONOUNCE it (in each regional dialect)! However, even this is not a universal absolute...because in Lokono-Arawak we have regional dialects & sub-dialects of our language, just as there are regional/national & sub-dialects of the English language.

Listen to the Queen of England speak English, then listen to a Scotsman, Welshman, Cornish person, 'cockney' Englishman, Canadian, American Australian, New Zealander, Guyanese, Jamaican, Indian, Kenyan, Nigerian, Trinidadian, Barbadian, Antiguan, Dominican, Grenadian, Vincentian, St. Lucian, etc etc - and you will hear ALL of them speaking a dialect of English - except the Queen and her ilk, only they speak perfect English closest to its oldest form.

So likewise, be cognizant of the fact that the Lokono in Venezuela, and the Lokono in Suriname, and the Lokono in French Guiana, and the Lokono in Guyana - all speak regional dialects (and sub-dialects)

- and they ALL have added foreign words to our language, which I have omitted from MY work here, so the reader gets only a PURE and ORIGINAL traditional Lokono language to learn.

The adding over time of foreign words was due to Colonialism and forced Christianization - with its cultural genocide essential tool of Eurocentric mis-education, by the Spanish & their language in Venezuela, the Dutch & their language in Suriname, the French & their language in French Guiana, and the English & their language in Guyana - where 75% of Lokono live & we are the biggest Tribal Nation in the country.

Furthermore - even a geographically insignificant distance like a mere 30 miles - which separates Pakuri Lokono Village and Moraikobai Lokono village in Guyana - is enough to result in noticeable differences, Pakurians find that their kin in Moraikobai speak very fast and pronounce a few words differently, whereas the Moraikobai Lokono find that their Pakurian kin speak slowly and pronounce a few words differently.

So anyone who tells you there is only one 'correct' way to speak and write Lokono - is telling you nonsense. This book is phonetically correct to the Pakuri (central Guyana) dialect, because it is one of the most genetically and culturally intact of all Lokono villages left on Earth, so much so - that it is referred to in academia as -'the cultural capital of the Lokono people', with 7 out of the 10 most famous Lokono persons on Earth - hailing from this one village of 1700 souls (nationally we are about 7,500 in Guyana).

I add a letter 'H' after almost every letter 'I' to many words so that you will know how to pronounce it correctly in Lokono. So instead of just writing ITABO I will write IHTABO, this is so you learn to always pronounce the letter 'I' as an 'ih' sound, not how the letter 'I' can be pronounced in English like it is in the word 'Lie' (just for example) , Some outsiders would even mispronounce ITABO (if I wrote it so) as 'EYE-TABO'.

Generally speaking there are two main and well known kinds of 'Arawaks' to non-indigenous people, in the minds of most outsiders these are the Taino (aka 'Island Arawaks'), and Lokono (Mainland 'Arawaks').

This book is not a dictionary of the Taino language, it is a dictionary of the Lokono language, or 'Toh Loko Ajeeaneewa' (the language of our people / the 'Arawak' language).

In our language, Lokono means 'the people' (of our tribe), and Loko means 'one person' (of our tribe). We Lokono are the only 'Arawaks' - that still live in semi-autonomous pre-Columbian territories with a culturally intact Chief and Tribal/Village Council system of government over our indigenous villages, the Tainos lost that and are trying valiantly to re-establish that, but it's a momentous uphill struggle bedeviled by ego and envy.

FOR EXAMPLE:

The National Police and Army of Guyana (where we are most numerous in terms of population and number of tribal villages and territories) have to ask our Lokono Chiefs for permission to conduct any activity on our territories, and they cannot arrest one of our people for a non-capital crime - if our Chief does not give them permission to do so, therefore we still enjoy a greater degree of traditional power, authority, tribal unity, and cultural cohesion - than our Taino kin in the islands, none of whom still have any officially recognised or demarcated Tribal territories, whereas the Lokono Territory of Pakuri in Guyana (where my wife is from and our children were born - and one buried), is 240 square miles of officially recognised and demarcated tribal land, even though we have only one village at the centre of it - with 1700 inhabitants, only 1% of which are non-Lokono. There are also dozens of other larger & smaller demarcated territories.

Infact, up until the 1970's Lokono men on Pakuri (fulfilling their traditional role as warriors loyally ready to fight at the side of our Chiefs) were still confronting outsiders who ventured uninvited up the 60 miles up the Mahaica River to our village, from Mahaica town on the coast - with bows and arrows (as ex-Chief Ernest Dundas told me), even though the Church has been active in our villages for almost 200 years and most of us have been wearing western clothes daily for over a century.

This is why many Tainos are looking to their Lokono kin to relearn aspects of their 'Arawakan' ancestral traditional cosmovision that they lost in the centuries of genocidal invasion and occupation of their homelands in the Greater Antilles.

Another important point to note, is that in neither the Taino nor Lokono language - does the word 'Arawak' actually exist, however we must face reality - and realize that 'Arawak' is the only word most non-indigenous people know to describe us, therefore we Lokono at least, have no problem with outsiders calling us Arawaks, because they genuinely do not know that we actually call ourselves Lokono in our own language, so why get all hot and bothered over it, we don't know the true names of most other peoples either, so no need for overly dramatic 'righteous indignation' when someone calls you by a name that they learned in some other peoples history books, being a jackass about it never helps.

Instead, we politely inform outsiders that our real name for ourselves is not Arawak, but is in fact Lokono, this informs the person who did not know - without insulting them - or being needlessly aggressive, as with our approach they leave with the impression that we are a friendly, peaceful, and intelligent people...however when you jump on an outsiders case and chastise them for an honest mistake like not knowing the name members of your tribe know for yourselves (and how they hell were the outsiders supposed to know that beforehand?) - the only impression you give - is that you are an aggressive ignorant jackass. As our elders say, you can catch more flies with honey than lime juice.

Even the Kalinago (aka 'Island Caribs' as opposed to the Kalina or 'Mainland Caribs'), have the same dilemma as our Taino kin, for there is not a single living Kalinago who can honestly say or prove - that they are still a fluent speaker of their own language, a few Taino are bold or crazy enough to claim they are, but they are only deceiving themselves and others with such fictitious claims.

However, when DNA and linguistic research was conducted on the Kalinago, we realised - and now consider them, to be our island kin too, because it was conclusively proven that in fact the Kalinago are genetically more Lokono than Kalina, no surprise as their pure Kalina male warrior ancestors migrated into the Lesser Antilles over 700 years ago, and they and their increasingly genetically diluted male descendants were taking Lokono women as wives for centuries, so naturally the paternal genes would be the minority now.

Although the Kalinago are the only ones in the Caribbean to still have a demarcated and officially recognised Tribal Semi-Autonomous Territory under the rule of a Chief and Tribal Council government, and it must never be forgotten - the Kalinago were NEVER conquered by any European Colonial power - not Spain, not Portugal, not France, not Denmark, and not England either, they held Dominica island against all odds.

We mainland Lokono were also never defeated by any European power in South America, they used us as paid mercenaries to suppress African slave rebellions, or fight other tribes, or other European colonial rivals, and this is a source of pride for all Lokono, even now they prefer us in the Jungle special forces of their modern day armies, because in battle we kill without mercy in all conditions, and we know the jungles better than anyone else.

SOME QUICK REFRESHER NOTES ON THE ABBREVIATIONS IN THIS BOOK:

N. = Nouns[1] are a person, place, thing, or idea. They can take on a myriad of roles in a sentence, from the subject of it all to the object

1. https://www.thoughtco.com/noun-in-grammar-1691442

of an action. They are capitalized when they're the official name of something or someone, called *proper nouns* in these cases.

Pron. = Pronouns[2] stand in for nouns in a sentence. They are more generic versions of nouns that refer only to people. Examples: *I, you, he, she, it, ours, them, who, which, anybody, ourselves.*

V. = Verbs[3] are action words that tell what happens in a sentence. They can also show a sentence subject's state of being (is, was). Verbs change form based on tense (present, past) and count distinction (singular or plural). Examples: sing, dance, believes, seemed, finish, eat, drink, be, became.

Adj. = Adjectives[4] describe nouns and pronouns. They specify which one, how much, what kind, and more. Adjectives allow readers and listeners to use their senses to imagine something more clearly. Examples: hot, lazy, funny, unique, bright, beautiful, poor, smooth.

Adv. = Adverbs[5] describe verbs, adjectives, and even other adverbs. They specify when, where, how, and why something happened and to what extent or how often. Examples: softly, lazily, often, only, hopefully, softly, sometimes.

Prep. = Prepositions[6] show spacial, temporal, and role relations between a noun or pronoun and the other words in a sentence. They come at the start of a prepositional phrase[7], which contains a preposition and its object. Examples: up, over, against, by, for, into, close to, out of, apart from.

---

2. https://www.thoughtco.com/pronoun-definition-1691685

3. *https://www.thoughtco.com/verb-definition-1692592*

4. *https://www.thoughtco.com/what-is-adjective-clause-1689064*

5. *https://www.thoughtco.com/what-is-adverb-1689070*

6. *https://www.thoughtco.com/preposition-english-grammar-1691665*

7. *https://www.thoughtco.com/prepositional-phrase-1691663*

Conj. = Conjunctions[8] *join words, phrases, and clauses in a sentence. There are coordinating, subordinating, and correlative conjunctions. Examples: and, but, or, so, yet, with.*

Interj. = Interjections[9] *are expressions that can stand on their own or be contained within sentences. These words and phrases often carry strong emotions and convey reactions.*

+ USE A THESAURUS TO CHECK FOR WORDS THAT HAVE THE SAME MEANING

ALL LOKONO WORDS END IN ONE OF THESE TWO LETTER EXAMPLES:

AA

AI

AN

AW

AY

BA

BO

CH

DA

DO

EE

---

8. *https://www.thoughtco.com/what-is-conjunction-grammar-1689911*

9. *https://www.thoughtco.com/what-is-an-interjection-1691178*

EN

EY

FA

FO

HA

HO

IA

IH

IN

JA

KA

KO

LA

LO

MA

NA

NO

NG

OA

OH

ON

OO

OY

PA

RA

RO

SA

SO

TA

TO

UA

UH

UN

WA

WO

YA

YO

YU

In the Lokono language there are NO sounds that correspond to the letters C, G, Q, X or Z - in the English alphabet.

For example, in English you can use the letter C or K often to get the same phonetic sound (Cat and Kit have the same K sound in the first letter), this is confusing so in written Lokono we only use one letter for this sound - which is K, the only way to honestly use a letter C in written Lokono - would be to put the letter H with it. So you can say in Lokono there is no letter C - only a CH sound.

So a Lokono Alphabet would actually be only 22 'letters':

A, B, CH, D, E, F, H, I, J, K, L, M, N, O, P, R, S. T, U, V, W, Y.

NB - Most animal and plant names in Lokono are deliberately left out of this dictionary, as it was created to assist more in you learning a basic conversational level, to learn all our names for Amazonian Flora & Fauna - I highly recommend my essential companion book to this dictionary, it is also written phonetically - but it also delves deeper into traditional Lokono spiritual cosmovision and culture than any other book ever written, and it is called simply 'Lokono Arawaks'.

If you want to know about our Myths and Legends and other supernatural folklore - my book called 'Amazonia's Mythical and Legendary Creatures in the Eagle Clan Lokono-Arawak Oral Tradition of Guyana' - will assist you greatly in that regard.

CHAPTER 2 - Letters A, B & C

A

A, or AN, adj. = ABA

Aback, adv. = ANAKOON

Abreast, adv. = KONIMA

Absent, adj. = KAWA

Abstain, v.i, = ORA

Abstinence, n. ORAHA

Accelerate, v.t. & v.i. = AWSABOKAN

According to, prep. = KONA

Accuse, v.t. = DISAKA

Accustomed, adj. = MOOTHEN

Ache, n. KAREEBEECHEE

Aching, adj. = KAREEBEECHEEHEE

Acid or Acidity, n = BORAHAHA

Accross, prep. = BAROODA

Actually, adv. = KEHBEH

Adjoining, adv. = OKOSA

Adultery, n. = BEEHEEROHA

Advise, v.t. = TOOKOODA

Affix, v.t. = DAYATA

Afraid, adj. HAMARO

After, adv. BENA

Afternoon, n. = BAKOOLAMA

Afterward, adv. = KENBENA

Again, prep. = KIBA

Again, adv. = IBA

Against, adv. = RABOODOOKOO

Aged, adj. = THOYO (a very old, venerable person - considered a living ancestor)

Ago, adv. = KOBA

Ague, n. = AWDASHAHA

Aim, n. = BUNATAHA

Aim, v.t. = BUNATA

All, n. = THOMAKOA

Allow, v.t. = AWTA

Almost, adv. = NIKWAN

Alms, n. = KOYABAHA

Along (with) adv. = KONABEECHEE

Alongside, adv. = ADANAN

Alongside, prep. = ROMAKONDI

Already, adv. = HEEBEE

Alright, v.i. = SANWAY

Also, adv. = BAJIA

Although, conj. = BARIKA

Always, adv. = IMEWABO

Am or Are, part of the verb 'to be', v.i. TOA

Amidst, adv. = KOBOROKODEE

Among, prep. = ONEKWA

Ancestors, n. = HEBEYONO

Anchor, v.i. = HATATOA

And, conj. = KEH

Anger, n. = KAIMA

Angry, adj. = KAIMAHA

Another, adj. = ABAABA

Answer, v.t. = ONABA

Anybody, pron. = HALIKAYRON

Anyhow, adv. = HALIKAJINRON

Anything, n. = HAMAARON

Anytime, n. = HALIKARON

Anywhere, n. = HALONDIRON

Apparel, n. = KONDO

Appearing, adv. = CHILEH-CHILEH-DAKWAN

Apply, v.t. = FITADA

Apportion, v.t. = LOKODA

Arawak, n. (one person of the tribe, or the language of the tribe) = LOKO

Arawaks, n. (many people of the tribe/the entire tribal nation) = LOKONO

Arched, adj. = DORAKA

Area, n. = KEELEE

Arise, v.i. = KANAKOA

Around, adv. = IRAJEE

Arrival, n. = ANDANTEH

Arrive, v.i. = ANDA

Arrow, n. = SHIHMARA

As, adv. = JIN

Aside, adv. = ABANROA

Ash, n. = BALISHEE

Ask, v.t. = ADAKOTA

Askew, adj. = OMADO

As much as, adv. = HALOMANTHO

As soon as, adv. = CHIHBIN

Assist, v.t. = BORATA

Assistance, n. = BORATAHA

Assume, v.t. = KIHSHIHKA

As usual, adv. = DOKA

At, adv. = AMOON

Attach, v.t. = LATADA

Attachment, n. = KAYWEHEE

Attractive, adj. = SAYBA

Aunt, n. = YABOWATHO

Awake, adj. = ANABA

Awash, adj. = SOBA

Awhile, adv. = NIMAN

Axe, n. (with head made of stone or shell) = BAROSA

Axe-handle, n. (made of wood) = BARODAYA

B

Baby (foetus), n. = ILONEE

Baby (male), n. = KORELIACHEE

Baby (female), n. = KORELIATHO

Baby-carer, n. = ILONEE-KIHTAKWANA

Baby-sling, n. = CHIHMEHEE

Back-pack, n. = WARIHSHEE

Backward, adv. = OOINAKANG

Backwards, adv. = OOINAKANRO

Bag, n. = SAAKA

Bail, v.t. = MAHARA

Bailer, n. = MAHARAHIH

Bait, n. = MENAHA

Bait, v.t. = MENATA

Bake, v.t = OOBOOSA

Bald, adj = MABARA

Bandage, n. = KOORAKWANA

Baptism, n. (naming of a child ceremony) = IHRIHTAHIH

Bare, adj. = MAWNAHA

Bark, n (a sound) = ELOKO

Basket, n. (made of Mookroo) = HABA

Basket, n. (made of Palm fronds) = WAYAREE

Basket, n. (elongated to strain cyanide out of bitter cassava) = YORO

Basketry, n. = DORAHA

Bathe, v.i. = AKAA

Bathe, v.t. = KIHDA

Bay, n. = DEBO

Beam, n. = BAHAYORA

Beautiful (female), adj. = SABANTHO

Because, adv. = ODOMA

Before, prep. = BURA (I came before you = DAI ANDA BEH BURA

Before, adv. = UBURA

Befoul, v.t. = SEKEDA (like if you farted in a room or made somewhere stink or filthy)

Befriend, v.i. = AYOTOA

Beg, v.i. And v.t. = KOYABA

Beggar, n. = KOYABARIN

Begin, v.t. = INATA

Beginning, n. INATAHA

Behind, adv, = AYABO

Behold, interj. = BAREN

Belch, v.t. = ARARADOA

Belief, n. = KIHDOOADAHA

Believe, v.t. = KIHDOOADA

Belongings, n. = ANIHKO

Below, adv. = ONABON

Bench, n. = ABALAA

Bend, v.t. TAMUDA

Beneath, adv. = FOODEE

Bent, adj. = LAMA

Best, adj. = SABOWABO

Bestir, v.i. = ROKOSA

Better, adj. = SASAWABO

Between, prep. = NAKANROKO

Between, adv. = BOKWAWA

Betwixt, adv. ANAKANROKO

Beverage, n. (any drink in general) = ATHAHA

Beware, v.i. = AYTHOA

Bewitch, v.i. = YAREMEDA

Big, adj. = FIHRO

Bigger, adj. = FIHRO-SABO

Biggest, adj. = FIHRO-WABO

Bile, n. (stomach acid) = SHIHFERO

Bind (tie up), v.t. = KURA

Bird-call, n = HANAKWA (also the name of a bird that makes that exact sounding call)

Bird-food, n. = TOKON

Birth, n. = URAYA

Birth-time, n. = URAYAKA

Bisect, v.t. (divide in half) = WALASA

Bit, n. (small piece of something) = SHOKOTHO

Bite, v.t. = ARADA

Bitter, adj. = SHIHFEH

Black, n. (color) = KARAMEH

Black-and-blue, adj. (skin bruise) = ORODOBA

Blackhead, n (pimple) = NONOLEE

Blackness, n. = KARAMEHIH

Blame, v.t. = DIHSAKA

Blame, n. = DIHSAKAHA

Blaze, v.i. = LOLDA

Blear-eyes (Red-eyes/Conjunctivitis), n. = YEBERO

Blind, n. (as in a hunters blind used to ambush game) = WABANEE

Blind, adj. = MAFA

Blood, n. = IHTHAY

Blow, v.t. And v.i. = FOODA

Blunt, adj. = MAMANA

Board, n. = DOROHA

Boast, v.t. = TOKWA

Boastful, adj. = TOKWAKA

Boat, n. (riverrain dugout canoe) = KANOA

Boat, n. (high sides ocean going large dug-out canoe) = KORIARA

Body, n (of a living creature) = IHFIHRO

Boil, v.t. = BOKA

Boil, n. (like a sore or abscess on your skin with pus in it) = SOOBUREE

Bone, n. = KABOONA

Bony, adj. = KABOONAHA

Bore, v.t. = OLAYDA

Borrow, v.t. = TANAABA

Bouyant, adj. (it floats) = YORA

Bow, v.i. (as in bow to show respect) = ODODOA

Bow, n. (the weapon) = SHIHMARABO

Bowl, n. = KUNKEE

Bowlegged, adj. = WALAKA

Boy, n. = IHLONCHEE

Bracelet, n. = DIHNASOHA

Braid, n. = KODAHA

Bramble, n (thorny bushes) = ADAKARARO

Branch, n. = DIRNABO

Break, v.t. = KAROODA

Breath, n. = AKOOBA

Breathe, v.i. = AKOOBAHA

Breathless, adj. = HEKEHEKERON

Brew, v.i. = FATA

Bridge, n. = CHIHMAKWANA

Bringing, v.i. = WIHRIATOA

Brittle, adj. = MEREHMEREH

Broil, v.t. = YABOODA

Broiled, n. (meat) = YABOODAHA

Broth, n. = OORA

Brother, n (in general) = BOODEE

Bubble, n. = FOORASA

Build, = AMARITAHA

Building, n. (like a traditional house) = BAHEE

Builder, = AMARIHTARIN

Bulge, v.i. = THOLADA

Bulky, adj. (means same a big/large) = FIHRO

Burn, v.t. = BIHCHA

Burst, v.t. = WAKADA

Bury, v.t. = KARATA

Buried, = KATA

Bushrope, n. = KAMORO

Bushy, adj, = CHIHBO

But, conj. (but I thought e,g) = THOMOROOA

Butterfly, n. (in general) = KAMBANA

Buttress, n. (of a tree) = DAHALAY

By, prep (by the way I ...) = NOMA

By, adv, (by way of the river) = BANDEE

C

Cackle, v.i. = KAKADWA

Call, v.t. = SHIHMAKA

Call, n. = SHIHMAKAHA

Calm, adj. = MUNDAWKA

Can, v.i. = KOMA

Cannibal, n. = EKEKULEE

Cap, v.t. = KWAMATA

Cape, n. (like a cape of land) = SHIHRIHMA

Capsize, v.i. = FAMOODWA

Care, n. = KAKOYA

Careful, adj. = KAKOYAHA

Carefully, adv. = KAKOYAKANIN

Cargo, n. = NAKARA

Carry, v.t. = ONAKA

Cat, n. (in general - any member of the cat family) = ARWA

Caulk, v.t. = SAKASA

Cave, n. (underwater) = BABO

Cave, n. (above ground) = SHIHBA BAHEE

Cease, v.i. = AYBOA

Celebrate, = HALIHKEBETOA

Cemetery, n. = KATANALAY

Central, adj. = ANAKUBO

Centre, n. = NAKAN

Ceremony, n. = ARIETO

Ceremonial, adj. = ARIETODA

Change, v.i. (into another being/shape-shifting) = EBESOA

Change, v.i. (change color slowly) = BOONARO

Character/Reputation = KISHITOA

Charcoal, n. = BOODAREESHEE

Chase, v.t. = KIHRDA

Chatter, v.i. = ARAYRAY

Chew, v.t. = SAKODA

Chewing, v.i. = YAMOOSA

Chief, n. (of one village) = KAFOTAY

Chief, n. (of a Chiefdom - of several villages) = IHSAW

Chiefdom, n. = IHSAWKA

Child, n. (male) = IHLONCHEE

Child, n. (female) = IHLONTHO

Childbirth, n. OORAEERAKA

Children, n. (humans before the onset of puberty) = IHRENO

Chip, v.t. (to chip food or wood etc) = FERODA

Choke, v.i. = TOKODA

Choose, v.t. = ONOOA

Chop, v.t. = ASOKA

Chop, v.i. = FARADA

Chubby, adj. = SHIHSHIHKA

Churn, v.t. = KOLOTA

Clan, n. = KOROBADO

Clan, n. (of non-Lokono) = BITHADO

Class, n. (a group of students) = MARIKONO

Claw, n. = KONA

Clay, n. = WAYA

Clean up, v.i. (an area) = EFODA

Clear, v.i. (an area of vegetation) = MAWKADA

Climb, v.i. = AMOODA

Climb, n. AMOODAHA

Cling, v.t = FITOA

Close, v.t. = TAKA

Clothe, v.t. (cover the skin) EKETA

Clothes, n. (that which covers the skin) = EKEH

Clubfoot, n. = HOOYOOBA

Clubfooted, adj = HOOYOOBUHA

Clumsily, adv. = ROMA

Clumsy, adj. = LOMPO

Cluster, v.i. = HORADA

Clustered, adj. = SEEREE

Cobweb, n. = ARAYAKILAY

Cockroach, n. = KAKALAKA

Cold, adj = MEEMEE

Colic, n. = ARADAHA

Collapse, v.i. = KOLEFEDOA

Colleague, n. = BIAMTHAY

Collection, n. = OOROOKOODAHA

Comb, n. = BAROODA

Comb, v.t. = BAROODWA

Comb, n. (of a bird) = SEPERAY

Come, v.i. = KOTHAY

Comet, n. = KEEHEEROWEEWA

Comfort, v.t. = AYKATA

Companion, n. = YOHO

Complicated, adj. = KAMUNCHINA

Complete, v.t. = EEBEEDA

Completed, adj. = HEEBEE

Complexity, n. = KAMUNCHINAHA

Composer, n. = BEYOOKA-BOOROOTARIN

Comprehend, v.t. = KAYADA

Comprehension (understanding), n. = KAYADAHA

Conch shell horn, n. = KAROPAIRA

Concealment, n. = YAKATAHA

Confess, v.t. = KAYADOA

Connected, adj. = BEEANDA

Consequently, adv. = KEEANA

Consider, v.t. = ONEKWAKA

Consume, v.t. = TOKA, or EKEH

Contented, adj. = HOROSHEE

Contentedness, n. = HOROSHEEHEE

Contents, n. = OLOKODO

Contrite (Sorry), adj. = NOKANAY

Converse, v.i. (speak with) = JIAJIADAWA

Convert, v.t. = EBESO

Cook, v.t. = ABOKA

Cook, n. = ABOKARIN

Core, n. (at the centre/in the middle of something) = OKOBA

Corner, n. = KOOWINA

Cost, n. = UYAWNA

Coughing, v.i. = THONDAHA

Cough, n. = THONDA

Could, v.i. = KOMA

Cover, v.t. = SHIFOTA

Coverlet, n. = BOKORO

Craving, n. = KAMUNASHEEHEE

Crawl, v.i. = LEBESA

Cream, n. = KOTHA

Creator, n. (God, Great Holy Spirit) = MAREECHEE-KWANCHEE

Creep, v.i. = ARWADA

Crispy, adj. = FOROFORO

Crop, n. = ROTAY

Crooked, adj. = TAMURAY

Cross, v.t. (cross a bridge etc.) = TIHMA

Crowd, v.t. = MABURADA

Crowd, n. = YOHORONO

CROWDED, n. = MABOORA

Crown, n. (Gold banded headdress) = KAROKOORI-OOKWAMA

Crumble, v.i. = MOROROSOA

Crumbly, adj. = FOOFOO

Crumbs, n. = EBAN

Crumpled, adj. = HOOCHEE

Crumple, v.t. = MOROROSA

Crush, v.t. = SARADA

Crust, n. = REESHEE

Crutch/Walking Stick, n. = LOKODEHEE

Cuff, v.t. = MOKORADA

Cultivate, v.t. = BIHKIHDOKOTA

Cup, n. = WASO or POTEH

Cure, n. = KALATAHEE or IHBIHNA

Cured, adj. = KALA

Curly, adj. = KAKAREE

Curse, v.t. = MIHRIHTA

Cursed, n. (a cursed place) = HAYTEE

Cursing, n. = AMIHRIHTAHA

Cursorily, adv. = THOOSHIHKONDIRON

Custom, n. (a tradition) = AMOOTHEN

Cut, v.t. = AROOKA

Cut, n. = ABIHKAHA

Cyst, n. = HEECHEEBAYA

CHAPTER 3 - LETTERS D, E & F

D

Dappled, adj. = BOOREEBOOREE

Damp, adj. = IHKOOIH

Dance, v.i. = IHBIHNAHA

Dance, n. = IHBIHNA

Dark, adj. = ORIHROKO

Dark-colored, adj. OORIHEE

Dark-colored male person = KAREMELEE

Dark-colored female person = KAREMERO

Darkness, n. = OREEROKOHA

Date (an appointment time), n. = KIHSHEE

Daughter, n. = OTHO

Daughter-in-law, n. = OTHIHO

Dawdle, (waste time, be slow) v.t. = DONADA

Dawn, n. = KASAKOHO

Day, n. = KASAKABO

Day (before yesterday), n. = MIYAKABWA

Day (after tomorrow), n. = MAWTHEBWA

Dead, n. = KABOOJAHA

Deaf, adj. = MAYKA

Dear (term of endearment) = LOLO

Death, n. = AYODAHA

Decayed, n. = THORONO

Decorate, v.t. = TOKOROTA

Deeds, n. = ANISHA (good deeds), also YALOKOTAHI (bad deeds)

Deep, adj. = TOLA

Deep-stitched, adj. = KATOKA

Deer, n. = KOYARA = bush deer, BEYOO = savanna deer

Defecate, v.i. = IHKEEYA

Defend/Protect = JINAMA KEN FARANG - literally means 'stand up and fight'

Deficiency, n. = FOONASHAHA

Deficient, adj. = AWKA

Definitely, adv. = BA

Defoliate, v.t. = MASADA

Degenerate, v.i. = BALIDWA

Dehydrate, v.t. = MARADA

Delay, v.t. = KIHYADA

Delicious, adj. = KAHAYA

Deliciousness, n. = KAHAYAHA

Dent, v.t. = SAPARODA

Denude, v.t. = MADISEDA

Deprive, v.t. = MEESHEEKEEDA

Depth, n. = TOTOLAHEE

Descend, v.t. = THOKODA

Descent, n. = THOKODAHA

Desert, n. MOOREE

Destroy, v.t. = ABOADA

Detain, v.t. = IHBENTA

Devastate, v.t. = MOTHODA

Devour, v.t. = ARADA

Dew, n. = ORARO

Diarrhoea, n. = SOREHEE

Dictate, v.t. = ANIHKIHTA

Die, v.t. = AHODA

Different, adj. = THONWA

Difficult, adj. = FARAY

Dig, v.t. = CHIHKA

Digging place (a mine) n. = CHIHKAAHA

Dilute, v.t. - ONAHADA

Diluted, adj. = ONAHA

Dim, adj. = TIHMIHRIHYA

Dine (to eat), v.t. = KOTA

Dining area, n. = KOTANALAY

Dip, v.t. = SWADA

Dirt, n. = IHREBEHEE

Dirty, adj. = IHREBEH

Disappear, v.i. = MAKAWADOA

Disapprove, v.t. = MOOTA

Discernible, adj. = HARONAHA

Discernibly, adv. = HARONAHAKWAN

Discontinue, v.i. = EBOA

Disgrace, n. = HABOORIHA

Dish (of food) n. = KOPERO

Disintegrate, v.i. = THOROKOODWA

Dislike, v.t. = MANSHEE

Dislocate, v.t. = FOOSHIHKA

Display, v.t. = OORAYATA

Dissolve, v.t. = THODA

Dissuasive, adv. = BARIN

Distance, n. = ANAKUN

Distant, prep. = ANAKUNRO

Distant, adj. = WAIKIHLEE

Distaste, n. = MANSHIHNIHEE

Distended, adj. = BOORIHSHEE

Dive, v.i. = MOOSHIDOA

Divergent, adj. = ABANRO

Divide, v.t. = KOLEBETA

Diving, n. = MOOSHEE

Do, v.t. = ANIHKA

Dog, (any pet canid, including a hand-raised fox - called WARERO) n. = AYOLEE

Don (to put on), v.t. = ALTADA

Done, adj. = IHDAY

Don't (Do not!), interj. = KAKA

Douse, v.t. = AYOTON

Douse oneself, v.i. = AYOTOA

Dove, n. = ADERI (pronounced A-DAY-REE)

Downwards, adv. = ABONRO

Drag, v.t. = DOOROODA

Drake, n (male Duck) = BOORARA

Drape, v.t. = KELEDA

Dread, v.t. = MOOTOA

Dream, (nightmare) v.i. = FAFADA

Dream, v.i. = TOOBOONEEYA

Dregs, n. = AYBAN

Dress, v.i. = KETOA

Dried, adj. = AWATOA, dried meat = JIHBALEH

Drift, v.i. = MALDA

Drink, v.t. = ATHAHA

Drip, v.i. = THABATA

Drizzle, n. REEBEEREEBEE

Drizzle, v.i. = REEBEETA

Droop, v.i. = YOLA

Droopy, adj. = YOLADWA

Drop, n. = THABA

Drought, n. MAKEERALEE

Drown, v.i. = THIHKAHAKA or CHIHKAHAKA

Drown, v.t. = TIHKAHAKOTA

Drowning place, n. = TIHKAHANALEE

Drowsy, adj. = TABOOSHA

Drum, n. = SAMBORA

Drunk (male), n. = SOMOLECHEE

Drunk (female), n. = SOMOLETHO

Drunken, adj. = SOMOLAY

Drunkenness, n. = SOMOLEHEE

Dry, adj. = SAKA

Dry, (to dry something) v.t. = WATA

Drying, n. = BOOHOOHDADA

Duck, n. = IHFA

Dugout canoe, (used in rivers and lakes) n. = KANOA

Dugout canoe, (used on the oceans & seas) n. = KORIARA

Dung, n. = IHCHEEKA

Dusk, n. = ORIHSAYBAY

Dust, n. = DARA

Dusted (Dusted with dirt) = KATHOOREE

Dweller (male), n. = YAHALEE

Dweller (female), n. = YAHARO

E

Each, adj. = NOMA

Eager, adj. = YORA

Eagle, n. = BARIRIA (pronounced BA-REE-REE-YA)

Earring, n. = JIHKEHEHEE

Earth (soil), n. = HORORO

Earth-inhabitants, n. = ONABOSAY

Earthquake, n. = ADOODOOSARO

Earthworm, n. = BAJEEREE, also BARAKARO

Eat, v.t. = ABOYOOA

Eatables, n. = THONAHA

Eater (of a specific kind of animal), n. = ARWATHAY

Eclipse (of the Moon), n. = KACHEE-ODON

Eclipse (of the Sun), n. = HADALEE-ODON

Edge (of a river or shore), n. = REFOOJEE

Edible, adj. = EKESHAMA

Education (learning), n. = AMAREEKOHA

Elders, n. = HEBECHONO

Electric shock, n. (from lightning or other natural phenomena) ASENDIHKIHTAHA

Embarrass, v.t. = ABOORIHTA

Embarrassment, n. = HABOORIHEE

Ember, n. = LARO

Embryo, n. = WIHREEYA

Employ, v.t. = EHMEKEBOTA

Emptiness, n. = MAWKAHA

Empty, adj. = MAWKA

Enamoured, adj. = KAIWAY

Encompass, v.t. = AKAWSA

End, n. = EBONWA

Ending, adj. = HARA

Ending, adj. (the pluralising suffix for all non-human words), = BAY

Enlarge, v.t. = FIHROTA

Enlist, v.t. = ONAKA

Enough, adv. = OMA

Entangle, v.t. = HATATA

Entangled, v.i. = TOKATA

Enter, v.i. = KODOA

Epilepsy, n. = BOOTHADOAHA

Equal, adj. = HOOROOKOO

Equalise, v.t. = HOOROOKOODA

Equivalent, n. = MANTHO

Erect, v.t. = JINAMAKOOTA

Escape, v.t. = AYKA

Escape, n. = ATOODAHA

Estuary, n. = OOYIMA

Evacuate, v.t. = OOLOOKOODA

Even if, adv. = BARIHNKEE

Event, n. = OBOORAN

Everywhere, adv. = THOOMAKWADIHRON

Exaggerate, v.t. = YAMOODOOKOOTA

Exasperasting, adj. = KAIMACHINA

Excessively, adv. = KAY

Exertion, n. = ROKOSAHA

Exhibit, v.t. = ADOKOTA

Exhibition, n. = ADOKOTAHA

Expel, v.t. = KOODA

Expensive, adj. = KAYAWNA

Expression, interj. = EMAY

Expulsion, n. = KOODAHA

Extinguish, v.t. = YAKOSA

Extract, v.t. = RAKASA

Eye-puss, n. = KOSERAY

Eye-wash, n. = KOBEEAHA

F

Faint, v.i. = BOOTHADOA

Fair, adj. = SAKEH

Fall, v.i. = TIHKIHDA

Fall, n. = TIHKIHDAHA

Family, n. = FOODOKOYOCHEE

Famine, n. = HAMOOSHAHA

Fan, n. = WAREE-WAREE

Fan, v.t. = WADA

Far, adj. = TAHA

Farm, n. = KOBAN

Fat, n. = IHKIHEE

Father, n. = IHCHEE

Father (term of respect), n. = AWA

Father-in-law, n. = MADOKOCHEE

Favourable, adj. = SAWKOO

Fear, n. = HAMAROSHA

Fearfully, adv. = HAMARON

Feed, v.t. = BOOYA

Feed, v.i. = KOTAKOTA

Female, n. = HEEYARO

Fever, n. = AWDASHAHA

Few, pron. = KABOONKAN

Field, n. = KABOOYA

Fight, v.t. = FARA

Fighter/Warrior, n. = FARARIN

Fighting/waging war/engaging in combat, n. = FARAHA

Fill, v.t. = IHBEKITA

Filth, n. = SEKEH

Filthy, adj. = SEKEHEE

Find, v.t. = AWCHIHKA

Fire, n. = HIHKIHHEE

Firebrand, n. = HIHKIHYOSHEE

Firestick, n. = KIHRIHKAHA

Firewood, n. = HIHKIHKODO

Firstborn, n. = SHIHRIHMA

First people, n. = KONAINO

Fish, n (in general) = HIHMEH

Fish, v.i (by using anaesthetic) = AYARIHDA

Fish, v.i. (by using hook and line) = BODEDA

Fish-hook, n. = BODEHEE

Fishing, n. = BEDEDAHA

Fishing-line, n. = BOODEHCHIHMEH

Fish-trap, n. = MASWA

Fist, n. = MOKORO

Fit, n. = OMA

Fitful, adj. = BOOTHABOOTHA

Fitting, adj. OOSA

Flame, n. = LOLO

Flap, v.t. = FADO

Flash, n. = THARO

Flat, adj. = SAPA

Flatten, v.t. = SAPADA

Flatulence/Farting/passing gas, n. = OKODAHA

Flavoursome, adj. = KAHOOYANEE

Flea, n. = KHAYAB

Fleetingly, adv. = KOONIHNANRO

Flesh, n. = SHIHROHKO

Float (the name for the Cassava-bread compactor) , n. = HESO

Float, v.i. = YORADA

Flog (to beat with a stick), v.t. = BOOROOKA

Flood, n = ONEBERA

Flourish, v.i. = BIHKIHDOA

Flower, n. = TOKORO

Flowing, adj. = MALA

Fly, n. = KODO

Fly, v.i. = AMORODA

Flying, adj. = AMOROTAHEH

Fold, v.t. = KOJIDA

Food, n. = KOTON

Food, n. (cooked) = ABOKAN

Food, n. (uncooked) = KOTAHA

For, prep. = BEEYA

Foreigner, n. = FARETHO

Foreman/Supervisor/headman, n. = AFOODEE

Forest, n. (Virgin) = ADABEH

Forest, n. (secondary) = KONOKO

Foretell, v.i. = AYCHIHKEECHA

Forget, v.i. = AYKASHA

Formerly, adv. = ABAHOON

Fornication, n. = UREHEE

Foster-child/Adopted child, n. = BIHKIHDARA

Foster-father/adopting father, n. = IHCHEEJEEANCHEE

Foster-mother/adopting mother, n. = OYOJEEANTHO

Fracture, n. = KAROODAHA

Fragment, v.t. = OOWALATA

Fragment, n. = OOWALA

Fragrance/perfume, n. = BOHOYAHA

Fragrant, adj. = BOHOYA

Frayed, adj. = PAPA

Friend (male), n. = BETHECHEE

Friend (female), n. = BETHETHO

Frog, n. = SHIHBERO

From, prep. = WAREEYA

Froth, n. = OKOTHA

Fruit, n. = ABOYOOAHA

Fruitless, adj. = ABOYOOAH-DEEYA

Fruit-tree, n. = DAKOOTHEH

Full, adj. = IHBEY

Fullfaced, adj. = AFOO

Fullmoon, n. = KACHEE-KOROBO

Fungus/Mushroom, n. = SEBIH-TETEH-ITCH

Futile, adj. AWSORO

Futilely, adv. = AWSORON

Futility, = AWSOROMA-RON

CHAPTER 4 - LETTERS G, H & I

G

Gait/Walk, n. = KONAHA

Game (edible wild animals), n. = DIHSAY

Game, n. = IHBIHRAHA

Game (the results of the hunt), n. = IHWIHEE

Garment, n. = EKEHEE

Gash, v.t. = AHADA

Gather, v.t. (to gather a bundle, or also gather a crowd of people) = OOROOKOODA

Gather, v.i. (to scrape things together like off the ground) = KARABASA

Gathering, (of people) = MABOORADA

Generosity, n. = IHRAHA

Generous, adj. = IHRAHA

Genuine, adj. = WABO

Giant, n. (supernatural) = YALOKO

Gift, n. = BOOKEE

Gill (of a fish), n. = KAYASANA

Girl, n. = IHLONTHO

Girdle, n. = AYDAKWANA

Give, v.t. = ASHIKA

Give-up, v.i. = ASHIKOA

Giving, n. = ASHIKAHA

Glad, adj. = HALIHKEBEH

Gladden, v.t. = HALIHKEBETA

Gladness, n. = HALIHKEBEHA

Gland, n. = KAHKEROKO

Glimmer, n. = KOOKOOEE

Glory, n. = KALEMEHA

Glowingly, adv. = LOROAKWAN

Glue, v.t. = FIHTA

Gluttonous, adj. = FOONA

Gluttony, n. = FOONAHA

Graw, v.t. = ROWAYDA

Go, v.i. = AWSA

God (Great Holy Spirit), n. = ADAYAHOOLEE

Gold, n. = KOROKOOREE

Good morning = KALIMANDO

Good afternoon, = BAKOOLAMAW

Good evening, = OREEKAW

Goodnight = OREEKADAWO

Goodness, n. = OOSAHA

Grandchild, n. = LIHKIN

Grandchildren (mixed sexes or males alone), n. = LESEYOCHEE

Grandchildren (females alone), n. = LESEYOTHO

Granddaughter, n. = LOOKUNTHO

Grandson, n. = LOOKUNCHEE

Grandfather, n. = DOHKOCHEE

Grandmother, n = KATHA

Grasp, n. = SAMOKOHA

Grasp, v.t. = KARAW

Grass (found in wet savannas), n. = DARASHIHREE

Grate, v.i. & v.t. = ANSA

Grater, n. = ANSAKWANA

Graze, v.t. = ARASA

Greater than, adj. = AJEE

Greeting,(in the morning time only) interj. = MOROKO

Grieve, v.i. = NAKAMODOA

Gripe, v.i. = SOO

Groan, v.i. = BEROSOA

Groan, n. = BEROSOAHA

Grope, v.i. = BEBEDA

Ground, n. = HORORO

Ground-itch, n. (skin rash), n. = TETELEEYOO

Grounds (dregs in a cup/discarded unusable remnants), n. = EFEH

Growth, n. = BIHKIHDAHA

Grow, v.i. = BIHKIHDAO

Guest, n (male) = KORIHAROCHEE

Guest, n. (female) = KORIHAROTHO

Gurgle, v.i. = FOORARA

Guts, n. = OOTEH

H

Hair, n. = BARAHA

Half, n. = ANAKIHJEE

Hammock, n. = HAMAKA

Handle, n. = DAYA

Handsome (male), adj. = SAKANCHEE

Hang, v.t. = YODOKOTA

Happy, = HALIKEBEH

Hard, v.t. = TATA

Harden, v.t. = TATADA

Harrow, v.t. = MOOKOOSA

Hasty, adj. = HIHTHEH

Hatch, v.i. = THORADA

Haul, v.t. = YOROKA

Haunt, v.t. = YALOKOTA

Have, v.t. = KAMOONKA

Hazardous/Dangerous/Unsafe adj. = BAHAYA

Head, v.i. = SHIHTA

Headbinder, n. = SHIHDIHKWANA

Headdress, n. = OOKWAMA

Headwork, n. = SHIHTAHA

Heal, v.t. = KALATA

Healed, adj. = KALA

Healthy, adj. = SAKWA

Hear, v.t. = KANABA

Heat, v.i. = KOMODOA

Heat, n. = THEREHEE

Heaven, n. (the spirit world) = AYONBANA

Heaviness, n. = KOODOOHA

Heavy, adj. = KOODOO

Help, v.i. = BORATOA

Helper/Servant, n. = SAANA

Here, adv. = YAHA

Hereabout, adv. = YAHANTHERO

Hiccup, n. = HOOKOOKOORISHAHA

Hide, v.t. = YAKATA

High, adj. = AYONG

High (in great altitudes), adv. = AYONDEE

Hit, v.t. = TADA

Hoard, v.t. = MUNTARA

Hold, v.t. = BOKOTA

Hole, n. = OHOLAY

Holy object, n. = SEMI (pronounced - SEH-MEE)

Holy man (Shaman, healer), n. = SEMICHI (pronounced SEH-ME-CHEE)

Home, n. = SHIHKOOA

Honor, n. = ADAYAKOOTAHA

Honourable, adj. = IHFIHLEE

Hook, v.t. = KOTOKOTA

Hook, n. = BODEH

Hookline, n. = WANTA

Hookrod (fishing rod), n. = BODEDAYA

Horn, n. = KOROPAYRA

Hot, adj. = THEREY

Houseroof, n. = BAHOOSHEE

How, adv. = HALIKAJIN

How are you? = HALEKWA-BA?

How are you folks? = HALEKWA-HA?

How are they? = HALEKWA-NA?

How is he? = HALEKWA-LA?

How is she? = HALEKWA-THA?

How many, adj. = FATA

How much, adv. = HALOMAN

Huddled, adj. = AWMANA

Hug, v.t. = ANAKA

Hull = MIHKIHSA

Hunger, n. = HAMOOSHAHA

Hungry, adj. = HAMOOSHA

Hunt, = AYOOKHAA

Hunter, n. = AYOOKHAARIN

Huricane, n. = HOORAKAN

Hurriedly, adv. = HIHTHENIH

Hurry, n. = HIHTHEHA

Husband, n. = REHCHEE

I

I, pron. = DA

Identical, adj. = KEE

If, conj. = FAROKA

Iguana, n. = YOOWANA

Ill, n. = ABOA

Illness, n. = ABOAHA

Image, n. = AYA

Image (an image), n. = YATAHA

Immature, adj. = WAJA

Immerse, v.t. = TOBADA

Impersonate, v.t. = KISHITOAKA

Implore, v.i. = KOYABOA

Imply, v.t. = CHIH

Imprint, n. = DIHKIH

Improve, v.t. = IHSADA

In, prep, = OLOKO (not in there = OORAKO, in there = IHRAKIH

Incapacitate, v.t. = KARAPASODA

Indistinct, adj. = MAFAKOAN

Inefficient, adj. = MAWIHDIN

Inert, adj. = KOROWA

Inexpensive, adj. = MAYAWNA

Infant, n. = KORELIA

Inflated, adj. = BOOROOSHEE

Inflict, v.t. = ANIHKIHTA

Inhabitants (of the spirit world), n. = AYUN-KONDIH

Inhabitants (natives of a place), n. = KONAINO

Inhuman, adj. = MALOKON (wicked, corrupt)

Injured, adj. = IHKORIH

Inside, n. = OLOKODIH

Insistent, adj. = MASHIKAN

Instead, adv. = KIHYAN

Instinctively, adv. = THEBENJIN (as a habit)

Intention, n. = TIHKA

Inter, v.t. = KATAH

Interfere, v.t. = AYORATA

Interference, n. = AYORATAHA

Into, prep. = OLOKO

Inverted, adj. = BOLOKA

Invisible, = MADIKISHAMA

Irritate (a wound), v.t. = KATA

Is, pron. = KAH

Island, adj. = KAIREE

Isolated, adj. = ABAMARIA

It (nominative case), pron. = TORA

It (accusative case), pron, = IN

Its (genitive of it), pron. = THA, THA-ANEE = It's own

Itchy, adj. = TETEH

Itch, n. (athletes foot) = HEBESEREH

CHAPTER 5 - LETTERS J, K & L

J

Jealous, adj. = SHIHMIHKA

Jealousy, n. = SHIHMIHKAHA

Jester/Clown/performing Comedian, n. = YOOROOBOODEE

Jettison/discard/throw/eject, v.t. = BOREDA

Join, v.t. = TAKA

Join, v.i. = KODONOA

Joist, n (horizontal structural member used in architecture) = BAYORA

Juicy, adj. = KARA

Jump, v.i. = DIHIHDAHEE

Jump, v.i. = DEE

Jump, (a sporting event), n. = DOOHIHDAHA

K

Keep, v.t. = IHKIHTA

Kick, v.t. = YAKASA

Kick, n. = YAKASAHA

Kill, v.t. = FARAA

Kin, n. = FOODOKOYOCHEE

Kindle, v.t. = KALEMETA

Kneel, v.t. = KOROSHIHBATOA

Know, v.t. = AYTHA

Knowledge, n. = AYNIHKO

Knowledgeable, adj. = AYCHIN

L

Labour, v.i. = EMEKEBO

Labour, n. (collective work) = MASHIHRIHMEHEE

Ladder, n (pole ladder - a log with steps cut into it) = TAROFO

Laggard, n. (slow-poke, idler. loafer) = MAHOOLORO

Lament,/Regret v.i. = YOOMOOYOOMOODOA

Lamp, n. = ALETEE

Land, v.i. = REBOTA

Land, n. (that is being used by someone already) = ORORA

Landing, n (canoe dock) = MOODAKULEH

Language, n. = AJEEANEEWA

Last, adv. = BALIKORO

Last night, n. = KASAKODABA

Later, adv. = TANOKESABO

Latrine/toilet/defecating spot, n. = IHCHIHKANALEE

Laugh, v.i. = IHMIHTHADA

Laxity/Indecision/Indifference, n. = MAWNORIHEE

Lay, v.t. = MEYODA

Laziness, n. = HOYEHEHEE

Lazy, adj. = HOYEHEH

Leaf, n. = ADABANA

Lean, v.t. = DOOLOODA

Leaning (against something), adv. = DOOLOOWAKWAN

Learn, v.t. = AMARIKOTWA

Learned, adj. = AMARIKO

Leathery, adj. = KIHRIHKIHREE

Leave, v.t. = OOYBA

Leave, v.i. = EYBWA

Leaves (used for eye wash), n. = WAROMOORIHKOBIA

Leaves (used to induce vomiting), n. = AYOMORADA

Leavings/remains/leftovers n. = OOYBAN

Left-side, n. = BAROMARIA

Leisurely/Relaxed, adv. - MENIHMENIHDAKWAN

Length, n. = WADIHEE

Lessen, v.i. = MAYOODA

Let, v.t. = YA

Lethargic, adj. = ASABAKA

Liana, n. (vine/bush rope) = BIHYAWRO

Liar (male), n. = MOORIHKACHEE

Liar (female), n. = MOORIKATHO

Liberal, adj. = IHRAHA

Liberate, v.t. = AWTIHKIHTA

Lick, v.t. BAYLADA

Lick, v.i. = BAYLA

Lid, n. = SHEFOTO

Lie, n. = MOORIHKAHA

Lie, v.i. = MOORIHKATOA

Lie (down), v.t. = ATOHRODA

Life, n. = KAKEE

Lift, v.t. = NAKIDA

Light (not heavy), adj. = THORA

Light, n. = KALEMEH

Lighted, adj. = LOLO

Lighten, v.t. = KALEMETA

Like, adj. = JIN

Likeness, n. = KIAJINKEE

Likewise, adv. = KIJIA

Limbless, adj. = MADOREH

Limping, = DIHIHDIHEE

Line, n. = TIHMEH

Linger, v.i. = IHBENTOAH

Liniment/Ointment, n. = LOOHOOTAKWANA

Living, n. = KAKINBO, 'will live' = KAKOOHA

Load/Cargo n. = NAKARA

Locality, n. = NALEE

Loin-cloth, n. = WERAKA

Loiter, v.i. = JIHNABADABONG

Long, adj. WADEE

Long (for), v.t. = BARIHTA

Long head being, the first lords of men, n. = WAJIHSHEE

Longing, adj. = KAMOONASHEE

Loose-fitting, adj. = FAHDOOFADOO

Lop, v.t. = THARADA

Lopsided, adj. = TIHWANAKOO

Lose, v.t. = BOREDA

Loud, adj. = KAKANIHKIN

Louse, n. = OOYEHEE

Love, n. = ANSHIHEE

Low, adj. = ONABO

Lower, v.t. = YOLADA

Lucky/Likeable, adj. = KANSHIHKINANG

Luminous, adj. = KALEMEH

Lying, adj. = MOORIHKA

CHAPTER 6 - LETTERS M, N & O

M

Maid-servant, n. = SANTHO

Mainly, adv. = BARIN

Make, v.t. = AMARITA

Malodorous, adj. HIHSHEE

Man, n. = WAJIHLEE

Manifestation, (Spiritual) n. = OORAYA

Manner, n. = KWAN

Man-servant, n. = SANCHEE

Manufacture/make, n. = AMARIHTAHA

Many, adj. = YOHO

Many (people), adj. = YOHOLEE

March, v.i. = LAILA

Marching, adv. = YEHKEE

Market-place, n. = YOKARANALEH

Marriage, n. AYKAHA

Married, adj. = AYKAH

Married person (newly/recently), adj. = AYKALIA

Married man (newly/recently), n. = AYKALIACHEE

Married woman (newly/recently), n. = AYKALIATHO

Married couple (newly/recently), n. = AYKALIALINO

Marrow, (bone marrow), n. = BOONALOKODA

Marry, v.t. = AYKA

Massage, v.t. = ALOOTA

Massage, n. = ALOOTAHA

Massage, v.i. = ALOOTOA

Master, n. = DAYNASHA

Mate (male), n. = AWSOKACHEE

Mate (female), n. = AWSOKATHO

Mature, adj. = HEBEH

Mature (for the age of the child) = ADAYAHA

Maturity, n. = HEBEHEE

May (an auxiliary verb - as in 'May I go out'), = BAKAH

Me, pron. = DEH

Meagre/pitiful adj. = WAKARA

Meal (a light snack), n. = KEROSAHA

Meal (specially prepared for travelling), n. = KOMANEE

Meal (of crabs, cassava starch and gravy), n. = KWAHARO

Meat (smoked), n. = JIHBAHLE

Meat, n. = SHIHSHIH

Medical expert (homeopathic medicine), n = IHBIHHIHDARIN

Medicate (using wild sage or Tobacco smoke and plants), v.t. = KOREDAH

Medecine, n. = IHBIHIH

Meditate, v.t. = KOROBOKOATOAH

Meet, v.t. = ANDAKA

Melt, v.t. = THODWA

Mend, v.t. = KAREMEDA

Meshed, adj. = WARAWARA

Middle, n. = ANOOKOOBO

Midget, n. = MOOJISHACHEE

Midnight, n. = KASAKODANAKAN

Migrate, v.i. = AYARODA

Migrated, adj. = AYARO

Mildew, n. = HADARAMAHA

Milk (breast milk), n = JORAHA

Mind, n. = KOROKOH

Mine, n. = CHIHKIN

Miss, v.t = KOOBOODAH

Miss, v.i. = KOOBOODAH

Mix, v.t. = ARANTA

Modest, adj. = KANIH

Mole (on the skin), n. = TEHBEH

Monotonously, Adv. = RIHBIHRIHBIHDAKWAN

Monster, n. = EMEMEH

Moon, n. = KACHEE

Moonless (night), n. = THOHROKONKA

Moonlight, n. = KACHIHKALEMEH

Moor/Dock/tether/tie-up a boat, v.i. = HATATWA

More, adj. = KEBEH-SABO

More, adv. = ABAKWAN

Morning,n. MAWCHA

Mortar, n. = HAKO

Mortar husband (the Pestle), n. = HAKORECHEE

Mostly, adv. = RONTHAY

Motionless, adj. = MAYAKWAN

Mother, n. = OYO

Mother-in-law (of a woman), n. = KEEREE

Mother-in-law (of a man), n. = MOOKOOTHO

Mother-in-law (of a couple's child), n. = SEROH

Mould, v.i. = DOROMA

Mountain, n. = HORORОSHEE

Mournful, adj. = NAKAMOO

Move, v.i. = ROOROOKWA

Mud/clay, n. = WAYA

Muddly, v.t. = KOOMOOKOODA

Multiply, v.i. = YOHOTOA

Munch, v.t. = KEROSA

Murky, adj. = KOOMOOKEE

Murmur, v.i. = ONOHODAH

Mushroom (edible), n. = SEBEE

Mushroom (poisonous - resembles an ear), n. = ADAJIKEH

Music, n. = BEYOOKAHA

Musical instrument (the bamboo flute), n. = BEYOOKA

Musician (player of the Bamboo flute), n. = BEYOOKARIN

Musician (player of the Bamboo flute and drum - the only traditional musical instruments, the Maraca is not an instrument it is a spiritual ceremony object), n. = AYKIHTARIN

Must, v. = LEE

My, pron. DAI

Myself, n. = DA-ONOOA

N

Naked, adj. = MERAKA

Name (call someone by their name), v.t. = ASAA

Name, n. = IHREE

Named, adj. = KIHRIN

Narrow, adj. = MABIHLOKO

Native (male), n. = KONJEE

Native (female), n. = KONDO

Natives, (the first people in this/that place), n. = KONAINO

Nearby, adj. and adv. = HOMOONEE

Nearly, adv. = HIHBIHRON

Neatly, adv. = SAREN

Necklace, n. = YEDEE

Need, n. = KANSHIHEE

Niece, n. = WUNTHO

Nephew, n. = WUNCHEE

Nest, n. = CHIHBOKO

Net (for fishing), n. = SHIHPEE

Net, v.t. And v.i. = ASHIA

Net, n. = ASHIAKWANA

Next, adv. = ADABOKORO

New, adj. = EMELEEYA

New-comer (male), n. = ANDOOLIACHEE

New-comer (female), n. = ANDOOLIATHO

Never, adv. = KIAFAYBARIN

Nibble, v.t. = KOOROOTA

Night, n. = KASAKODA

Nightmare, n. = FAFADAHA

Night spirit, n. = WIHJIHLEE

No! Intel. And adj. = BAKOO

Nobody, n. = HALIHKANKORO

Nodule, n. THOYAHA

Noise, n. = KAKANOOKOOHA

Noisily, adv. = AWAKWANA

Non-bather (person who does not bathe 2x daily like a normal person), n. = MAKANRO

Non-person, n. = MELOKO

Nonsensical, adj. = AWSORON

Noon (midday), n. = WAMHADALEE

No-one, pron. = HALIKAIKORO

Not, adv. = KOROH

Notch, n. = RIHRIHTA

Nothing, n. = HAMAKORO

Now (today), adv. = TANOHO

Now (this instant), adv. = KAROHO

Nudge, v.t. = FOOYOOTA

Numb, adj. = MABARO

Number, n. = KIHSHIHDAHA

Nurture (young animals & humans), v.t. = BIHKIHDA

Nurture (young plants), v.t. = BORODA

O

Oar, n. = REMO

Observatory (place where the elders look at the heavens), n. = DOOKOOSHIANALEH

Observe, v.t. And v.i. = DOOKOOSHA

Occaission, n. = ABAHOONKIHBA

Occaission, adj. = BWAKA

Occasionally, adv. = BWAKANOMA

Odour, n. = EHEROHA

Odiferous/smelly.stinking, n. = HIHSHIHRO

Of = DAY

Off-shoot, n. = BOROH

Often, adj. = IHMENEE

Oftener/more often, adj. = IHMESABO

Oh! Interj. = AKOY

Oil (from animal fat, trees, etc), n. = OOLEE

Old, adj. = WAHADO

Oldness, n. = HEBEHA

Omen, n. = AJIBAHA

Omit, v.t. = EYBA

On, prep. = OKONA

Once, adv. = ABAHA

One, pron. = ABARO

Only, adj. = ROON

Opaque, adj. = KOMOOKEE

Open, v.t. = THOROA

Openly, adv. = THOROAKWAN

Opposite, adj. = OLABOA

Or, conj. = NOSO

Or, prep. = BATA

Outdoors, n. MAWKIHLEE

Ova, n. = WIRIA

Over-there = TAHARO

Overcut, v.t. = SHIHROKOTA

Overpower, v.t. = MOOTA

Overshadow, v.t. = AYABOTA

Overturn, v.t. = FAMOODA

Owner (male), n. = KANIHCHEE

Owner (female), n. = KANIHTHO

CHAPTER 7 - LETTERS P, Q & R

P

Pack, v.t. = SHIHSA

Paddle, n. = NALEHEE

Paddle, v.t. = NAKATOA

Paddling prowess, n. = NALEKABO

Pain, n. = KARIHIH

Painting, n. = YATAHA

Paint stick, n. = YATAKWANA

Painful, adj. = KAREE

Palate/taste, n. = BADARA

Pallid/pale (in skin complexion), adj. = HEHEH

Pantry/food storage area, n. = KOTONALEH

Parasite, n. = ADATIHMA

Parboil, v.t. = KOLASA

Parcel, n. = JIHKIHTAHEE

Parcel, v.t. = JIHKIHTA

Parch/roast, n. = KORODA

Parrot, (in the Macaw genus in general), n. = MAKAH

Parrot, (in the Amazon parrot genus), n. = BOOLTERO

Partner, n. = BIAMTHEH

Pass, v.t. = BALEE

Passable, adj. = IHSAH

Past, n. = WAKIHLEE

Past, adv. = BALIKA

Paste, v.t. = SEPEDA

Pathway, n. = BOONAHA

Peace, n. = MAYAWKA

Peaceful, adj. = MAYAW

Pebble, n. = SHIHBAKARO

Peel, v.t. = SODA

Peel, v.i. = SODOA

Peep, v.t. = DOOKOOSHA

Penetrate, v.i. = YAKOA

Person/Human being (of our tribe), n. = LOKO

Persons/Human beings (of our tribe), n. = LOKOBEY

People, (some other people), pron. = ABAROOKONO

People (many people of our tribe, our tribal nation as a whole), n. = LOKONO

Percolate/filter, v.t. And v.i. = YAKWA

Perfect, adj. = HIHBIH

Perhaps/maybe, adv. = JIARO

Perhaps so, adv. = JIAROKEE

Person in charge/Headman, n. = AFOODEE

Personality, n. = WAYAA

Perspiration, n. = ADOOBOOCHIHEE

Perspire, v.t. = ADOOBOOCHIHTOA

Pet, n. = LIHKIHNEE

Pick, v.t. OYA

Pick-up, v.t. = BOOTA

Pierce, v.t. = KIHTA

Piles/Hemorrhoids , n. = YOTORO-ESEREH

Pinch, v.t. = SOOKOORIDA

Pith, n. = TOOLA

Plait, v.t. = KODA

Plant, (in general), n. = KRATA

Plant, v.t. = BOONA

Plate, n. = KAROBO

Platform (for storing food in a house or over a fire to cook it), n. = BAROBAKOOA

Play, v.i. = BIHRA

Play, v.t. = IHBIHRA

Play (a musical instrument - bamboo flute or drum), v.t. = EYKIHTA

Player, n. = IHBIHRARIN

Play area (for toddlers), n. = SOORA

Plaything/toy, n. = BIHRAKWANA

Please, v.t. = IHSAYKATA

Pleased, adj. = IHSAYKATOA

Plough, v.t. = THAMUDA

Ploughing, n. = THAMUHA

Pluck, v.t. = THIHKIHDA

Plump/chubby, adj. = HIHBIHRO

Point, v.t. = KIHLIHKA

Point, (of land) n. = SHIHREE

Poisoned, adj. = IHBIHSHA

Poison-tree, n. = HIAREE

Polisher (a smooth stone), n. = ROHOHO

Pond, n. = KIHRAHA

Poor, adj. = KAMOONAIKA

Porridge, n. = KOYAREE

Port, n. = AMOODAKOOLEH

Portage/Haul/Hoist, n. = TIHMANALEH

Portend/Foretell/Predict, v.t. = AJIBA

Portent, n. = AJIBWAHA

Portion, n. = IHBENA

Portray, v.t. = OYATA

Possibly, adv. = JIAROKEE

Post, n. = BAHIHSEH

Postpone, v.t. = IHBENTA

Pot (big clay cooking pot), n. = DWADA

Pound, v.i. = IHTA

Pour, v.t. = SONKA

Pour, v.i. = SONKOA

Poverty, n. = KAMOONAIKAHA

Powdery, adj. = TIHLEE, also KATHUHREE

Practically, adv. = HIHBIHKEHBEH

Precisely, adv. = KEEYAREN

Precocious/Cocky, adj. = AWIDEE

Predict, v.i. = AYCHIHKIHTA

Preferable, adv. = WATO

Premonition, = AYTHAA

Presence, n. = OMAKANA

Present, v.t. = BOKITA

Presently, adv. = TANOKEH

Preserve, v.t. = SALARODA

Preserve, n. = SALARO

Pretend, v.t. = TWAKA

Price, n. = YAWNA

Principle, n. = HIHSHIHA

Print, n. = BOREE

Privation,/Hardship, n. = DAFOOAHA

Probable/Possible, adj. = MANTHAN

Probably/Presumably, adv. = JAROBAHA

Probe for, v.i. = KOROTA

Prod/Nudge/Press v.i. = THOLATA

Profanity/swearing/cursing, n. = MIHRIHTAHA

Projection/Extension, n. = TOREH

Proliferate/Breed/Reproduce, v.i. = REPEDA

Promiscuous, adj. = OREH

Propagate, v.t. = HEMEYODA

Prosper, v.i. = FAFASOA

Protect/Defend = JINAMA KEN FARANG (literally means 'stand up and fight')

Provocative, adj. = KAYMACHINA

Provoke, v.t. = AYMATA

Pry/Poke, v.t. = MIHRIHKA

Pulverise, v.t. = FOROTA

Purchase, v.t. = AYAWNTA

Push, v.t. = CHIHRIHKIHDA

Push, v.i. = KOROTA

Q

Quick, adj. = KAHOOLOO

Quickly, adv. = MEHERAN

Quiet, n. = MEEAW

Quietness, n. = MOONDAWKAHA

R

Rainbow, n. = ALAAMOOLOO

Rain, v.i. = IHKIA

Rain, n. = ONEE

Rainfall, n. = KOREYNARO

Rank (smell), n. = KASHEE

Rash, adv. = HIHTHEH

Rather, adj. = THOREH

Rations, n. = KALEH

Rave, v.i. = YAWDA

Raw, adj. = OOYA

Really, adv. = WAA

Reap, v.t. = WADAHEE

Reckon, v.t. = KISHADA

Recover, v.i. = KALATOA

Red, adj. = KOREH

Red-eye (Conjunctivitus), n. = KOREKOSHEE

Region, n. = AWKIHLEE

Rejoice, v.i. = HALEKEBETOA

Relapse, v.t. = SAKADA

Relapse, v.i. = TIHKADOA

Relation (female elder), n. = TAYTAY

Relation (male relative), n. = YOHOCHEE

Relation (female relative), n. = YOHOTHO

Relatives, n. = YOHONO

Remain, = EYBA

Remainder, n. = EYBAN

Remember, v.t. = KOROKWA

Remove, v.t. = RIHRIHKA

Repellent, adj. = KEHEH

Replenish, v.t. = KWOOYBA

Reproachful, adj. = KARIKONATHO

Resemblance, n. = YAH

Resembling, adj. = JAMARO

Resentment, n. = KAYMAHA

Return, v.i. = KOYWA

Reveal, v.i. = KARAYA

Reverse, v.i. = KOOYKIHTA

Reverse, v.t. = SHIFODA

Ridge, n. = SHIDO

Right (opposite of left), adj. IHSA

Right-side, n. = IHSAMARIA

Ripening, adj. = HAYBAYBO

Rise, v.i = ANAKIDWA

Roaring, v.i. = OMADA

Roast, n. = YABODA

Rock (anything made of stone), n. = SHIHBA

Rock, v.t. = YODA

Rock, v.i. = YODOA

Roll, v.t. = ORIHBIHSA

Room, n. = KAMBARA

Roost, v.i. = BOLOLOTWA

Root, n. = OKORA

Rope, n. = KAYORO

Rosy, adj. = HOBO

Rotate, v.t. = SHIHRIHBIHDA

Rotten, adj. = THORO

Rouse, v.t. = KOROKODA

Route, n. = BOONAHA

Ruler, n. = (a Chief with authority over 2 or more Chiefdoms), n. = AHAROKO

Rump, n. = IHIHTORA

Run, v.i. = DARIHDA

Runner, n. = DARIHDARIN

CHAPTER 8 - LETTERS S, T & U

S

Sag, v.i. = YOLADOA

Sage (wild Amazon sage), n. = AYTHAKIHLEE

Saliva, n = KWEE

Salt, v.t. (to salt meat, or fish etc.) = KABATA

Salt, n. = PAMO

Salt-container, n. = PAMOKEH

Salty, adj. = KABA

Same, adj. = KEE

Sand, n. = MOTOKO

Satiety (feeling full after eating or drinking), n. = HOROSHIHA

Satisfaction, n. = HOROSHIHEE

Satisfied, adj. = HOROSHEE

Satisfy, v.t. = HOROSHIHDA

Savings (anything deliberately left back for future use), n. = MUNTARA

Savings (food leftovers), n. ROHOTA

Savour, v.t. = KAHOOYATA

Savoury, adj. = KAHOOYA

Say, v.t. = AH

Sayer, n. (male) = MALEE

Sayer, n. (female) = MARO

Scab, n. = OODATAREH

Scald, v.t. = CHIHDA

Scald, n. = CHIHDAHA

Scare, v.t. = BOKA-OOYA

Scare (yourself), v.i. = BOKO-AWYA

Scared, adj. = MOOTOA

Scatter, v.i. = ATHABAA

Scatter, v.t. = LAKADA

Scattered, adj. = TAHADEE

Scattering, n. = ATHABAHA

Scoop, v.t. = SHIHLAKA

Scorch, v.t. = BIHTAKA

Scorn, v.t. = YAYMADA

Scrape, v.t. = FOORIHSA

Scraping, n. = FOORIHSAHA

Scratch, v.t. = KARASA

Scribe, n. = ABOOROOTALEE

Scrub, v.t. = SARADA

Sculpture/woodcarving, n. = YATAHA

Sea, n. = BARA

Seashore, n. = BARA-REBO

Seaside, n. = REFUDEE

Search, v.t. = WAHADA

Search, n. = AWADAHA

Season, n. = KACHEEKA

Season (dry), n. = MAKIHRALIHKAA

Season (wet), n. = YOOYAWKA

Second-growth forest, n = MAINAP

Second-growth area, n. = IHBIOKIHLEE

Secure, v.t. = IHSADA

Sediment, n. = ORO

See, v.t. And v.i. = ADOOKA

Seek, v.t. = AWADA

Self-conscious, adj. = HABOOREE

Selfish, adj. = HIHKIAHA

Selfishness, adj. = HIHKIAHAHA

Selfsame, adj. - KIAKEE

Send, v.t. = IHMIHKODA

Sense, n. = YENIKOHA

Sensitive, adj. = SOOLOOSOOLOO

Separate, adj. = ABAADEE

Separate, v.i. = ABAMARIA

Servant, n. = SANA

Servants, n. = SANANO

Serve, v.t. = KOOIHBA

Sew, v.t. = KOOSA

Sewing, n. = AKOOSAHA

Shake, v.t. = FADAKODA

Shake, v.i. = FADOKODWA

Shallow, adj. = MATOLA

Sharp, adj. = KAMANA

Sharpen, v.t. = MANTA

Shelf, n. = YORADA

Shell, v.t. = BARAKASA

Shelter (made with a leaf roof), n. = BENAB

Shelter, v.i. = ADOTOA

Shine, v.t. = KALEMETA

Shines, v.t. = KEYENDA

Shiny, adj. = KALEMEH

Shiver, v.i. = KOROKOSA

Shock (as from an electric eel), v.t. = ASENDIHKIHTA

Shoot, v.t. And v.i. = AYOOKA

Shoot (of a plant), n. = FOOREE

Shop (the act of looking for things to barter for), v.i. = BAKOTA

Shore, n. = REBO

Short-statured, adj. = BESEKEN

Shoulder, v.t. (as in you had to shoulder a load/carry a burden), = NAKATOA

Shoulder, n. = DIHNAINA

Show, v.t. = DOKOTA

Shower, v.i. LAKADOA

Shred, v.t. = PAPA

Shredded, adj. = PAPADA

Shriek, v.i. = TEREKEDA

Shrivel, v.i. = SAWA-YODWA

Shrivelled, adj. = SAWAYO

Shut, v.t. = TAKA

Side, n. = MAREEYA

Sideways, adv. = ROMAKONA

Sifter (for Cassava flour), n. = MANAREE

Sift, v.t. = YOOBOOSA

Signal, v.i. = IHKIHSHIHTOA

Signal, n. = IHKIHSHIHTOAHA

Silence, n. = MAYAKWAHA

Silent, adj. = MOONDA

Silently, adv. = MAYAWKWAN

Similar, adj. = MANJIN

Similarly, adv. = KIHJIARIHKIHKEE

Simmer, v.t. = ABOKOTA

Since, conj. = WANA

Sing, v.t. = YENTUA

Singing, n. = YENTUAHA

Sink, v.i. = KONA

Sister (older), n. = YORODATHO

Sister (younger), n. = JIHKIHDO

Sister (a twin), n. = BOORADO

Sister-n-law (of a man), n. = OOROONAYTHO

Sister-in-law (of a woman), n. = ORIHBIANTHO

Sit, v.i. = BALTA

Sizzle, v.i. = SOOLOOKOODA

Skeleton, n. = ABOONAAROON

Sketch, v.i. And v.t. = YATA

Skin (of an animal), n. = WAYAY

Skin (of a human), n. = YEDA

Slap, v.t = FATADA

Slash, v.t = MASHIHRIHMEDA

Sleep, v.i. = ADONKA

Sleepy, = TABOOSHA

Sleeplessness, n. = ANABAHA

Slender, adj. = SWAREH

Slice, v.t. = DABARETA

Slide, v.t. and v.i = TELEKEDA

Slime, n. = KOYELEE

Slimy, adj. = KOYEH

Slip, v.i. = ROTA

Slippery, adj. = TELEHTELEH

Slow, adj. = BASADA

Slowly, adv. = BASADAN

Slumber, n. = ADONDAHA

Slush, n. = ROROLEE

Slushy, adj. = KOPEH

Small, adj. = SHOKO

Small, n. (male) = SHOKOKIHLEE

Smal, n. (female) = SHOKOKORO

Small (young plants), n. = IHBEE

Small-man (a friendly term in the tribe), n. = SHOKOCHEE

Smeary/dusty adj. = KATHOREE

Smell, v.t. = JIHMIHSA

Smell, n. = EMEH

Smelly, adj. = HAMOOYAHA

Smoke, n. = KOREHELEE

Smoke (meat), v.t. = JIHBALEDA

Smooth, v.t. = MOOYAMOOYA

Smoulder, v.t. = LAROSA

Snare (a bird trap), n. = TARAMPA

Sneeze, v. i. = CHEDA

So, adv. = KEE

So, (as in 'like so') = DAYKEEA

So, conj. (so therefore) = DAYBA

Soaking, adj. = KOLO

So far, adj. = BARIN

Sorcery (evil spiritual work), n. = YAREMEHEE

Soft, adj. = BELEH

Soggy, adj. = SOSO

Soldier/warrior, n. = FARARIHN

Some, adj. = ABAA

Something, n. = HAMATHALEE

Some time, adv. = HALIHKAJIHARO

Sometimes, adv. = BOOAKANOMA

Somewhat, adv. = KO

Son, n. = AYCHEE

Son-in-law (of a man), n. = ORIHTHECHEE

Son-in-law (of a woman), n. = CHIHCHEE

Sons (in general), n. = ACHIHNO

Sons (a term of endearment), n. = AYCHIHNOCHEE

Song, n. = YENEE

Sound, n. = THOOLEE

Sound, v.i. = KANOOKOOTOA

Sour, adj. = BORAHA

Source, n. = SHIHROKO

Sour-liquid, n. = BORAHARO

Spacious, adj. = KABOORA

Sparse, adj. = DARADARA

Speak, n. = AJEEYA

Speaker, n. = AJEEYARIHN

Specialist, n. = ARIHN

Special, adv. = WAYTO

Speckled, adj. = BOOROOROO

Speech, n. = AJEEYAHA

Spherical, adj. = BALALA

Spill, v.t. = SONKOTA

Spin, (palm leaf or agave straw on your thighs) v.t = ORODA

Spinning, n. = ORODAHA

Spirit animal, n. = BIHSOOREE

Spirit, n. (evil and non-human entity) = YAWAHAA

Spirit, n. (malevolent human spirit that lingers on the Earth) = MASHIHSHIHKIHREE

Spirit, n. (non-malevolent human or animal spirit) = KOYAHA

Spirit-arrow, n. (energetic arrow send to kill enemies) = YAWAHOO-SHIHMARA

Spit, v.i. = KOOYDA

Spite, n. = BAKOKOAHAA

Spiteful, adj. = BAKOKOA

Spittle, n. = ORARON

Splash, n. = TAKAY

Splashily, adv. = THAY

Splinter, v.t. = IHLOKOSA

Splutter, v.i. (accidentally take in water through the nostrils) = MOORIKA

Splutter, n. = SOOLOOKOODAHA

Spoil, v.t. = BALIDA

Spoon (wooden) n. = LEPELEH

Spoon (made from a gourd), n. = HARARO

Spoon (Large wooden and for stirring the big clay pot only), n. = KARARAHA

Spotty, adj. = PARAPARA, a Jaguar is also called 'FIRO PARAPARA ARWA' which means 'big spotted cat'.

Sprain, v.t. = HOOYOOBOODAKA

Sprain, n. = HOOYOOBOODAHA

Sprained, adj. = FARASA

Spread, v.t. = FIHLADA

Spread-eagle, v.t. = WALAKADA

Squal, n = SOOROOBOOKOOLEE

Squat, v.i. = BOROTAY

Squatting, adj. = BOROTEHKOAN

Squeeze, v.t. HOOIHDA

Squint, v.i. And v.t. = SHIHKIHRIHDA

Squint-eyed, adj. = SHIHKIHREE

Squirt, v.t. And v.i. = SHIHRAKADA

Stale, adj. = SASA

Stalk, v.t. = BEROA

Stampede, v.i. = RESWA

Stance, n. = JIHNAMAHA

Stand, v.i. = JIHNABA

Stand up and fight = JINAMA KEN FARANG (same expression means defend or protect)

Star, n. = WIHWA

Star (the morning Star), n. WAROKOMA

Stars, n = WIHWABAY

Starlight, n. = WIHWAKALEHMEH

Starch, n. = HARO

Start, v.t. = OOYNATA

Startle, v.t. = MAYADA

Steal, v.t. = KACHAYKAYBAY

Steer, v.t. = BOKODA

Steersman, n. = BOKODARIHN

Step-daughter, n. = TABOATHO

Step-son, n. = AYCHIHBOACHEE

Step-father, n. = THEBOACHEE

Step-mother, n. = OYOBOATHO

Stick, v.t. = CHADA

Sticky, adj. = TEBEYO

Stiff, adj. = TATABOODEE

Stiffen, v.t. = TATABOODITA

Still, adv. = KWAN

Sting, v.t. = THIHDA

Sting, n. = SHIHDAHA

Stink, n. = HIHSHIHEE

Stink-out (the place), v.t. And v.i. = HIHSHIHDA

Stir, v.t = KARADA

Stoke, v.t. = KODOTA

Stone, n. = SHIHBA

Stool, n (traditional low carved wooden stool) = ABALA

Stooped, adj. = HODO

Stooping, v.t. = DORADA

Stop, n. = THOKODONALEH

Stop-off, n. = SPAREE

Straight, adj. = MIHSHEE

Straighten, v.t. = MIHSHIHDA

Strand, n. = RAWREH

Stranger, n. = NONO

Stranger to the world (referring to a new born baby), n. = NONOSA

Stray, v.i. = BOREDOA

Strike, v.t. = KORATA

String, n. = TAU

Strip, v.t. = ABA

Stub, v.t. = KATADA

Stuff, v.t, = SHIHSA

Stumble, v.i. = AROTAKA

Stumble and stagger, v.i. = FETODA

Stump, (also stub) , v.t. = KATADA

Stun, v.t. = BOOTHADA

Stunted, adj. = PASHIHMA

Stuntedness, n. = PASHIHMAHAA

Substitute, n. = DIHKIHLOKO

Suck, v.t. = SOWTA

Sucker, n. = BIHSHEE

Suddenly, adv. = ABAREN

Suddenly limp, adv. = THOYA

Suicide, v.i. = FAROA

Suitable, adj. = SAKEN

Sun, n. = HADALEE

Sunlight, n. = HADALEE-KALEHMEH

Supervisor/Headman, n. = FOODEE

Supplication, n. = OKONARIA

Suppose, v.t. = KIHSHIKA

Supposedly, adv. = THA

Supposed to, v.i. = THA

Surrender, v.i. = ASHIKOAKA

Surroundings, n. = KIHRAJEE

Swallow, v.t. = MOOKOODA

Swamp, n. = BAWKIHLEE

Swarm, v.t. = KOROKODA

Sweat, n. = ADOOBOOCHIHEE

Sweat, v.t. = ADOOBOOCHEE

Sweaty, adj. = ADOOBOOCHIHTA

Sweep, v.t. = SOOROOBOODA

Sweet, adj. = SEMEH

Sweetness, n. = SEMEHEE

Swelling, n. = KEKEROKOHA

Swift, adj. = KAHALAY

Swiftly, adv. = RIHSA

Swim, v.t. = CHIHMA

Swoon, v.i. = YAO

T

Tail, n. = IHHEE

Tail-feathers, n. = LAWHAA

Take, v.t. = ANAKA

Take-off, v.i. = NAAKIHDOA

Talkative, adj. = KAJIANKABONEE

Tall, adj. = ADAYBAYRA

Tallness, n. RAYAKONAHA

Tame, adj. = MAKOYA

Tandem, adv. = KAYNABAN

Tangle, v.t. = TOKATA

Taper, n. BOOKOOROOHA

Teach, v.t. = AMARIHKOTA

Teacher, n. = AMARIHKOTARIN

Tear, n. = KIHRA

Tear, v.t. = THOOROOKOODA

Tearful, adj. = AYCHEE

Teenager (male), n. = BIHKIHDOLIACHEE

Teenager (female), n. = BIHKIHLIDOLIATHO

Tell, v.t. = AAKA

Temperature, n. = THEREHAA

Temptation, n. = KIHSHIHDAHA

Tend, v.t. = AWOONTA

Tender, adj. = MOROMORO

Term of respect for elders, n. = BEHBEH

Territory, n. = HORORO

Test, n. = KIHSHEE

Test, v.t. = KIHSHIHDA

Thanks, n. = DANKEE

That, (dem. pron.), = TORAHABO

That, (dem, adj.) = TORAHA

That way, = TADIBO

The, pron. TOH

There, adv. = YARABO

Their, pron. = NA

Them, pron. = DAI

Then, adv. = OOKA

They, pron. = NAI

Things, adj. = ABAROOKO

Think, v.t. = CHIHNRON

Think, v.i. = KOROKOTOA

Thirst, n. = HALAKOSHAHAA

Thirsty, adj. = HALOKOSHA

This, dem. adj. = TOHO

This, dem. Pron. (this one) = TOHOBO

This coming, adv. = ANDABOTHEKORO

This way, adv. = YADIHBO

Thorn, n. = KIHTOOKA

Thorns, n. = KOOTOOKABEH

Those (males), dem pron. = NERAHA-MUNCHEE

Those (females), dem. Pron. = NERAHA MUNTHO

Though, conj. = BARIHNKEE

Threat, n. = YADAHAA

Threaten, v.t. YAADA

Thrive, v.i. = FAFASWA

Throb, v.i. = BORATA

Through, adv. = OLOKODEE

Thunder, n. = KORAKALEE

Thus, adv. = TOHOJIN

Tickle, v.t. = MOOROOMOOROOTA

Ticklish, adj. = MOOROOMOOROO

Tie, v.t. = KEERA

Tight, adj. = HEEREE

Time, n. = KA

Tipsy, adj. = KATHOOSHIA

Tiptoe, (to tiptoes) = THAYRAYBAYTWA

To, prep. = MUN

Toast, v.t. = MEHREHMEHRETA

Toasted, adj. = SAREH

Tobacco, n. = YOOREE

Today, n. = TANOHO

Tomorrow, n. = MAWCHEE

Tonight, adv. = TORIHKA

Too, adv. = KEMA

Top, adj. = AJEEAKO

Top-heavy, adj. = OMADO

Topple, v.i. = ADOLADOA

Torment, v.t. = DAFOODA

Touch, v.t. = BEBEDA

Towards, prep. = RONRO

Towards dawn, adv. = KASAKOMAREEYA

Town, n. = BAHYOHO

Toy, n. = BIHRAKA

Toy/Handle/Use (with someone or something), v.t. = MENIA

Trail, n. = SOORIHEE

Trample, v.t. = TOONABO

Trap, n. = EREH

Trap, v.i. = EREDA

Trapper, n. = EREDARIHN

Travel, v.i. = YADA

Tray (made of basketry), n. = BEEHEE

Tread, v.t. = TIHNA

Tree, n. = ADA

Tremor, n. = RAKASAHA

Tribe, n. = KIHRIHKIHYA

Tributary, n. = ONIHKAN

Trickle, v.t. = SOROKODA

Trouble, v.t. = AYORATA

Trough, n. = ADIHSA

True, adj. = KIHDWAHAA

Trunk, n. = OODAYA

Truth, n. = KIHDWAHAA

Try, v.i. = KIHSHIDOA

Tuber, n. = ODOOLEE

Tubers (plant bearing a lot of), n. = KADOOLINO

Twin (non-human), n. = IHBEEYO

Twin (human), n. = MONOOSHEE

Twitch, v.i. = LOOKOOSA

U

Ulcer, n. = ESEREH

Ultimate, adj. = HARA

Uneven, (place of uneven ground) = TIWANAKO

Unable, adj. = MAMAREE

Unnavigable, adj. = MATOLA

Unbecoming, adj. MAMOODAN

Uncle, n. = DINCHEE

Underdone, adj. = IHEYA

Underneath, adv. = ABON

Underneath, prep. = AFOODEE

Under-parts, adv. = ABONDEE

Undying, adj. = MAYAKOSONTHO

Unfinished, adj. = MIHBIHDIN

Unfamiliar, adj. = EMELEEYA

Unloose, v.t. = DOKODA

Unlucky, adj. = MANIHKABO

Unripe, adj. = IHMORO

Unsound, adj. = MIHSA

Unstable, adj. = LAMALAMA

Untamed, adj = KAKOYA

Untidy, adj. = WAKAWKA

Untie, v.t. = DOKODA

Uprightness, adj. = MISHIHI

Uproot, v.t. = DOLADA

Uproot, v.i. = DOLADWA

Upwards, adv. = AYONRO

Urinate, n. = DAKA

Urine, n. = EHEHI

Useless, adj. = MAMENIANTHOMA

Usually, adv. = NOMA

Us, = WAI

CHAPTER 9 - LETTERS V, W & Y

V

Veer (off from), v.i. = HAWREDA

Very, Adv, = BANDEE

Very, (this very one). = KENTHOHO

Vine, n. = DOWOKWAROYOWA

Visit, v.i. = ADOOKA

Visitor (who is a friend), n = KORARIHEE

Vomit, n. = EWAYDA

W

Wadding, n. = WARAKA

Waggle, v.t. = THEREBEDA

Wait, v.i. = ABADA

Wait, n. = ABDAAHAA

Wake, v.t. = ANABIHKIHTA

Walk, v.i. = KONA

Wall, n. = TAKARSA

Want, v.t. = KANSHEE

Want, n. = KANSHEEHEE

War, n. = FARAAHA

Warrior, n. = FARARIN

Warm, v.t. = KOMODA

Warm, adj. = WEREBEH

Warmth, n. = WEREBEHEE

Warn, v.i. = KOYATA

Wart, n. = WAYSO

Wary, adj. = KAKOYA

Was, = WA

Wash, v.t. = ASOKOSA

Water, n. = ONEEABO

Waterfall, n. = ONEEABOCHIHKIHDIN

Waterless, adj. = MAKOORA

Water-mark (high tide mark), n. = KATARA

Water-spirit, = OREEYO

Waterway, n. = IHTABO

Wattle, v.t. = YARA

Wattles, n. = YARADA

Wave, n. = HOROMOOREH

Wavelette, (small waves/ripples), n. = SHIHBA-SHIHBARO

Wax, n. = KARIMAN

We/Us, pron. = WAI

Wealth, n. = ADAYAROHAA

Wear, v.t. = OKONA

Weariness, n. = METHEHEE

Weary, adj. = METHEH

Weave, v.i. = DORA

Weep, v.i. = AYA

Weeping, adj. = AYTEE

Weeping, n. = AYAHA

Wet, adj. = YOOYOO

Wet season,n. = YOOYAWKA

Wet, v.t. = YOTA

What, pron. = HAMAHA?

When, adv. = HALIKA

Whenever, adv. = HALIHKAKEE

Whensoever, adv. = KATOKA

Which, adv. = HALIKANBO

While, adv. = MANKA

Whimper, v.t. = THEDOA

Whip, n. = MAKWAREE

Whirlpool, n. = KAYAMOO

Whiskers, n. = CHIHMA

Whisper, v.t. = THETHEDA

Whisper, n. = THETHEDAHA

Whistle, v.i. = HOHIHDA

Whistle, n. = HOHIHDAHAA

White, adj. = HARIHRA

Whiteness, n. = HARIHRAHAA

Who, adv. = HALIHKANG

Who, pron. = HALIHKAI

Whoever, pron. = HALIHKAIJIALEE

Whosoever, pron. = HALIHKANWATHO

Wicked, adj. = WAKAYA

Wickedness, n. = WAKAYAHA

Wide, adj. = BIHLOKO

Widen, v.t. = BIHLOKOTA

Widening, n. = BIHLOKOTAHAA

Widow, n. = BOTOBATHO

Widower, n. = BOTOBALEE

Width, n. = BIHLOKOHA

Wife, n. = RAYTHO

Will, v.t. = MOOKOOTA

Willing, adj. = IHMEKO

Willingness, n. = IHMEKOHA

Wilt, v.i. = WAYLIHDOA

Wilted, adj. = WAYLEE

Wind, n. = AWADOOLEE

Wink, v.i. = YABOOSA

Wink, n. = YABOO

Winkingly, adv. = YABOOSAHAA

Wipe, v.t. = RAWDA

Wisdom, = LEETAHAMATALEE

With, prep. ABO

With, pron. = OMA

Woman, n. = HIHYARO

Wonder, v.t. = BAHA

Wood-gathering (collecting firewood), v.t. = SOORIDA

Work, v.i. = EMEKEBO

Work, n. = EMEKEBOHA

Worsen, v.t. = TIHKADOA

Wound, n. = IHKORIHEE

Wound, v.t. = IHKORIHDA

Wrath/Anger/Rage, n. = AYMA

Wrestle, v.i. BOREDA

Wrestler, n. = BOREDARIN

Wrestling, n. = BOREDAHAA

Wring, v.t. = SAMORODA

Wrinkled, adj. SAWARA

Y

Yard, n. = SOWKIHLEE

Year, n. = IHWIHWA

Yellow, adj. = SOBOLEH

Yes, int. = EHEY

Yesterday, n. = MEYAKA

Yet, conj. = KEEYAKEE

Yonder, adj. = YAKOOTAHA

You (singular, nominative case), pron. = BAY

You (singular, objective case), pron. = BOO

You (plural, nominative case), pron. = HEYBAY

You (plural, objective case), pron. = HOO

Young, n. (immature), = MOOROOMOOROO

Young, adj. = BIHKIHDOLIA

Young plant, n. = BOONAKARAHEE

Younger (brother), n. = DIHKIHDEE

Younger (sister), n, = DIHKIHDO

Youngsters (humans), n. = IHBIHROBEH

Your, pron. = BA

Youth (male), n. = BIHKIHDOLIACHEE

Youth (female), n. = BIHKIHDOLIATHO

Youth (in general), n. = IHLONEE

Don't miss out!

Visit the website below and you can sign up to receive emails whenever Damon Corrie publishes a new book. There's no charge and no obligation.

https://books2read.com/r/B-A-ADZI-BTESB

Did you love *A Phonetic English to Arawak Dictionary*? Then you should read *Lokono-Arawaks*[1] by Damon Corrie!

2

This book is the most comprehensive phonetic compilation of cultural information ever produced about the Lokono-Arawak Tribal Nation, of north-east Amazonia, a must-have publication for any academic, Taino, or Kalinago person wanting to know more about their Arawakan ancestral heritage and re-learn some basic practical aspects of their tangible and intangible heritage.

After spending his entire life researching as much information as he could find from as many sources as he could find, about his own Lokono-Arawak people, the author realized that there are very few, less than 5 books of first-hand direct source information ever published that were written in English by a Lokono-Arawak person, and 2 of

1. https://books2read.com/u/barMJQ

2. https://books2read.com/u/barMJQ

those were written by him, and the others were by pro-assimilation Lokono who did not reveal half of their ancient traditional spirituality that the author has revealed here for the first time.

So the author decided to finish this project – to write a general knowledge comprehensive book about the Lokono-Arawak people, that he actually started 27 years ago, however it was a long and slow process of accumulating notes here and there, now and then but never finding the time to compile all in one volume. This is where the COVID-19 Pandemic became a blessing in disguise, becoming unemployed and with nothing but time on his hands, finally gave the author the 4 months he needed to put it all together.

Most Lokono-Arawak persons alive today have passed through the scorching fire of Colonialism and its heir – Neo-Colonialism, and much of the information contained in this book – they are themselves unaware of because what was not beaten out of their grandparents and parents in Colonial-era Eurocentric schools, was preached out of them via the other fist of European colonialism called 'Religion'....where the so-called 'representatives' of God on Earth – reinforce the brainwashing of indigenous peoples to make them believe that whatever the non-indigenous priest/pastor tells you is 'Godly and true', but whatever your Tribal Holy man tells you is 'a lie from the Devil'.

So this inter-generational trauma has left most of the Lokono alive today under 50 years old very ignorant of much of what is revealed in this book, and very much trapped in the lingering mental slavery Colonial-era brainwashed pro-assimilation thinking that only what the Europeans say or do – is 'civilized' and 'progressive'....and whatever the pro-traditionalists like the author say or do – is 'uncivilized' and 'backward'. So this book was designed to become a tool to ignite a spark in their hearts and souls, to not just claim to be 'proud indigenous' with empty words and put on a show once a year at Heritage month time (September in Guyana – the precise month this book was released), but to TRULY live by those words, and begin to re-learn what it is to be a Lokono-Arawak again, and begin to forget what it is to live like an imitation European – as most are still doing to this day.

This unique bok was also created to help Taino and Kalinago tribal relatives of the Lokono-Arawaks, because they have lost more of their traditional society from this terrible era of Eurocentric domination and forced assimilation, with not a single fluent speaker of either of their respective languages left alive today. This book can become an invaluable resource to any Taino or Kalinago who truly seeks to rediscover their ancient roots. Lastly, this book will become an invaluable academic resource for all dedicated researchers of indigenous cultures worldwide.

Read more at https://www.facebook.com/shamanchief/.

Also by Damon Corrie

Life Lessons Series

Understanding Spirituality, Anomalous Phenomena as life lessons

Understanding Spirituality, Dreams, Insights, Exorcisms, Visitations and Shamanic Healing

Dream State Experiences

Standalone

The Amazon is Burning - The Flames of 21st Century Resistance Inspired by Indigenous Women

Amazonia's Mythical and Legendary Creatures in the Eagle Clan Lokono-Arawak Oral Tradition of Guyana

Lokono-Arawaks

The Last Arawak girl born in Barbados - A 17th Century Tale

Confessions of a Reiki Exorcist

A Phonetic English to Arawak Dictionary

Watch for more at https://www.facebook.com/shamanchief/.

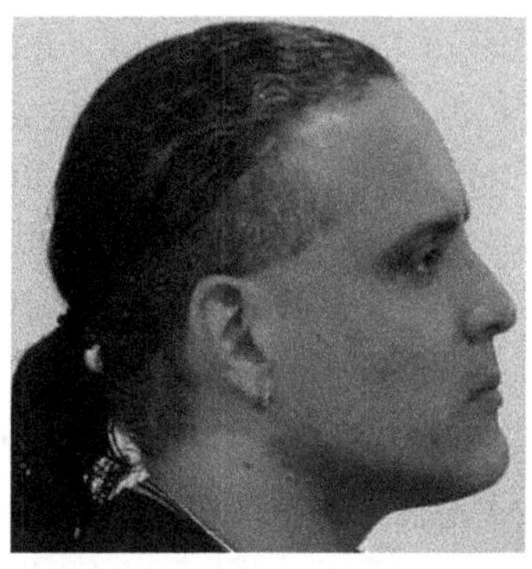

About the Author

Damon, like his 3 older siblings, was born on the Caribbean island of Barbados. His mother Audrey named Damon after the American author Damon Runyon, and from a very young age Damon exhibited a passion and love for writing; however, like most aspiring authors Damon found it impossible to share his manuscripts with a broader audience (until he discovered draft2digital), so for over 3 decades his many works in many genres gathered dust on his bookshelf of unfulfilled dreams.

Damon is a 4th generation descendant of the last traditional Hereditary Shaman Chief Amorothe Haubariria (Flying Harpy Eagle) of the Bariria Korobahado Lokono (Eagle Clan Arawaks) of Guyana, South America, Moreover, the grave of Damon's great grandmother is the only known burial site of a member of Lokono-Arawak nobility in the entire Caribbean - and with a tombstone written in both the English and Lokono-Arawak language, it has become a tourist attraction in the Westbury Cemetery in the capital city of Bridgetown Barbados.

Damon has the gift of premonition dreams and being able to see and communicate with deceased loved ones, and since he married back into the tribe at the age of 19 in 1992, Damon has become the most radical indigenous activists the Caribbean has produced in living memory, and his real-life escapades and supernatural experiences feature in his writings.

Damon was a member of the Caribbean Caucus on the Indigenous Peoples working group of the Organization of American States (OAS) from 2000 to 2016, and helped create the Declaration of The Americas on the Rights of Indigenous Peoples, and he has been a registered participant of the United Nations Permanent Forum on Indigenous Issues (UNPFII) since 2007 (where he also co-mentors international students and writes for the Tribal Link Foundation), as well as being an autodidact journalist with news articles published in 4 continents, and a writer for the Last Real Indians indigenous media website.

Damon (46) and his wife Shirling (44) have 4 living children, sons Hatuey Francis (26) and Tecumseh Shawandase (23), and daughters Sabantho Aderi (20) and Laliwa Hadali, and all live in Barbados. Damon can be followed in Instagram @eagleclanarawaks

Read more at https://www.facebook.com/shamanchief/.

About the Publisher

www.ingramcontent.com/pod-product-compliance
Ingram Content Group UK Ltd.
Pitfield, Milton Keynes, MK11 3LW, UK
UKHW021657190726
13853UKWH00001B/322

9 798201 102036